This author is a licensed child care provider and has written the book based upon her personal experiences. This book's purpose is to provide information on the topics covered. It is sold with the understanding neither the author nor the publisher is engaged in rendering legal, financial accounting, or other professional services. The author doesn't assume any liability resulting from action taken based on the information included herein.

Always consult an accountant, tax preparer, or your state child care licensor for the most accurate information on the business of home daycare.

Contents

Chapter 12 Forms/Examples   Page 74-107

Introduction

This book is for people who are looking for a rewarding career in the home daycare industry. It includes tips on how to open and successfully operate a rewarding business in the comfort of your home.

<u>Chapter One</u>

~ Opening Up A Family Daycare ~

Congratulations on taking your first step towards a career that is both rewarding and financially sound. With the economy being as unpredictable as it is, this is one job that remains in high demand. Families *need* to earn a living and relying on good childcare is a necessity. *Home* daycare is becoming more popular, mainly because of the high cost of expensive child care centers. Now is the perfect opportunity for you to start your own business, set your own hours, earn a decent living, and save on the many costs associated with working outside of your home.

If it's so easy, why isn't everyone staying home and doing it? Hey, don't get me wrong, this career can be very challenging and the hours long. But if you love children and are willing to do what it takes to make your business successful, than this is an excellent option for you. Not only will you be your own boss, but you will reap the rewards financially.

How do I know all of this? From personal experience. I *am* a successful daycare provider who loves the freedom of being her own boss and earning a great income. Life is good. But this wasn't always the case. Before I did this my career consisted of fifty plus ho

Let me tell you, it took some work to get started. I didn't know anyone in the business and went in with my eyes closed. There were many speed bumps along the way and I learned most of the things *after* the children were in my home. One of the most essential things I found out after starting this new adventure was that it takes certain personal traits to make a home daycare successful. These include extreme patience, creativity, flexibility, and really caring about other people's children. Not just caring for them but caring *about* them.

As I've said, I'm still running my own daycare and I earn a decent living. Watching ten children can bring an upwards of $65,000 to $70,000 a year in my area. Plus I'm home with my children and I am my own boss.

This book is designed to help you reach your goals successfully and to avoid the many mistakes which many providers make during their first year, causing them to give up and quit. These are true methods that work and I still use them today.

Now, before we get started there are some very important questions to ask yourself; do you enjoy being around children for long periods of time? You will be surrounded by the little angels for 10-12 hours a day and if you do not have the willingness, patience and the tolerance you will certainly not succeed. Children will test you and push you to the limit. It's important that you keep your cool and your temper in check.

Also consider these points:

Home sweet home? What was simply your home is now a place of business. Parents and children will be coming and going. The serenity of your home will now be an amusement park for the little angels you will be caring for. Things will get broken, lost, and bitten apart. Anything and everything that is out will take some wear and tear. Walls, carpeting, furniture, and things you would never consider will get damaged. Be prepared and don't be surprised when it happens. Childproofing your home is one of the first steps to keeping both your children safe as well as your belongings.

Your Children. This will definitely affect your whole family. Young children must share their space, toys and their parent. Some kids adjust but others dislike the whole idea. There will be bouts of jealousy and your older children may even react by being bossy or super sensitive. Be open and communicate to your kids that the attention you are giving the others does not mean you love them less. I usually communicate many times throughout the day how much I love and appreciate them.

Your Husband or Partner. Generally your other half will be very supportive to opening up a daycare. Unfortunately as time goes by and they find their home is not what it was, it can be very frustrating for them. It may take time for them to adjust and sometimes they can't. Before opening up a daycare you should really sit down with them and weigh the benefits against the negatives of opening one up. Be realistic about the changes and what will be going on in your home; long days, wear and tear on your home, dirty diapers, strange smells, and lots of chaos at times. If you can, it's a very good idea to try and keep your main living area separate from your daycare. Everyone will benefit in the long run.

Potty training. You will be responsible for assisting with that. There will be many accidents throughout the day, even from some of the older children at times. You will go through many rolls of toilet paper, wet wipes, and soap. Some children take longer than others to train and it will be challenging. There is also another growing problem called Encopresis. Children holding their bowel movements (usually because they have had painful ones in the past),causing blockage and eventually soiling themselves uncontrollably. I had two children that came into my care with this problem. You *can* work with the parents to get through this, although it can take time and a lot of patience.

Pets. You may need to keep your pets separate from the children. Not only to keep the children safe but to keep your pets safe as well. Children love animals, especially pulling on their tails or using them as a "horse" to ride on. And of course more children have allergies as well, so keeping them away during the day might be the best choice.

Smoke-free. Under no circumstances are you allowed to smoke around the children. You have to be in their presence all day. If you can't go ten hours without a cigarette, then you should quit smoking before you start watching them or consider choosing another career.

Cooking. Can you cook? Do you like to cook? You will be responsible for providing nutritious meals and snacks for the kids. Forget frozen pizzas and canned meals. Home cooked meals are what is expected from you. Fortunately there are some great government funded food programs that you can join which will not only give you some great advice on food preparation, and may also help fund your meals. We will talk about this later in the book.

Room. Do you have the room to run a daycare? Is there room for six to twelve children to play comfortably? Will they be tripping over everyone? Is the bathroom accessible to the play area? Where will the children eat? Do you have a big enough backyard or outside play area for the children to release their energy? If there is a pond or lake near, by you will need to have it fenced in. There are many things to consider and we will get into some ideas later in this book.

Skills. There are many skills that are required even in daycare. Are you a good communicator? Do you have the skills to multitask? Are you good with arts and crafts? Being organized with your paperwork is also a very important skill.

Can you run a business? Running your own daycare means you are self-employed. You need to keep accurate records and be very organized. If you are comfortable with doing so, we will go through more information on this later in the book.

Chapter Two

~Why Some Daycares Fail~

Not having clear policies

Make sure that you have a handbook and contract with very specific information. Detail everything including when you should be paid to what holidays you will be closed. If you do not point out the days you are closed, you will have parents showing up at your door and will be responsible for watching them.

In the back of this book is an example of a basic Handbook. Make sure that you create one and have your parents take them home. Whenever you come across something you may have missed in your handbook, add it. Handbooks and contracts are a necessity for having a successful Daycare.

Lack of Support from Partner and Children.

Some partners can't stand the site of toys cluttered and the loud noise and racket of children playing or leaving at the end of the day. And sometimes your own children have a tough time dealing with sharing their parents as well as their own toys. It's important to have boundaries. Your children need their own toys as well as space from the daycare. Keep their bedrooms off limit if at all possible and make sure you shop for separate toys. You can find great deals at garage sales as well as Craig's List. I found a lot of "free stuff" on Craig's list to help me with supplying my daycare.

Too Many Children At Different Age Groups.

Nobody mentioned this to me when I was starting out, I learned it the hard way. If you are a new provider and are watching two infants, a toddler, two preschoolers, and five school age children, expect a lot of chaos. I filled my daycare right away with different age groups and found it very difficult to juggle everything by myself. Two infants that needed to be changed and fed every couple of hours; toddlers and preschoolers who needed one on one attention with art projects and learning activities; fighting among the school aged children. Preparing the breakfasts, lunches, and of course all of the snacks. Talk about stress!

Now I was able to juggle everything eventually, but it wasn't easy. Having a daily schedule of when you expect to do everything really helps, but don't rely on it. Infants do not understand schedules, and parents seem to waver a lot on their own. It seemed like the infant's parents never had a "set timeframe". I'd expect them before the school aged children, but some days they would arrive late without even a phone call. This can really throw your schedule off when you are trying to get the snacks ready for the older children and suddenly the infant needs a bottle.

The more experienced providers have learned to either stick with a similar age group, especially if you plan on providing a preschool curriculum, or hire an assistant. If you put too much on your plate, you may find yourself giving up on the entire business by feeling overwhelmed. Start slowly and add on as you become more comfortable.

To get a better picture of how to run a successful daycare, visit a well established provider. Most of them are busy but still friendly. Try to visit when the children are present and see how they have laid out their daycare. Most of them will have a daily schedule of different activities for the kids. Have a list of questions for them. What types of challenges do they face? What is their background? And is there anything she or he recommends for starting out? It's important to know as much as you can before the first child sets foot inside of your home. You will certainly get a better sense of what you are setting yourself up for by visiting a provider than by just reading about everything.

Chapter Three

~How and Where to begin~

Check with your state to find out how to obtain your license. Social Services is generally the department that regulates child care. They may have you sign up for some type of orientation which will outline the steps needed for the license. You can also check with the National Association of Family Child Care at 801-269-9338. They should be able to forward you to the right offices.

To obtain a license you will generally need to take some type of classes before you are approved for daycare. In Minnesota I needed to get certified in CPR, First Aid, SIDS, Shaken Baby Syndrome, and Child Restraints. You will get the information from your state which will outline what is needed and where you can take the classes. I spent less than $150 on all of the classes that I needed to take and did it in one month. If you are serious about getting licensed, sign up for the classes as quickly as possible, they usually fill up quick.

Licensing

There are different kinds of licensing (usually small and large) and each state may have a different capacity allowances. When I started out in Minnesota, for the first year I could have up to ten children, with only six being non-school aged and less than three under two years old. This was considered a smaller license. This is specifically for Minnesota. Each state and even county will have their own type of regulations. You will be responsible for learning what they are. Never compare them to another state or even county. Find out what yours is and make sure to abide by those rules or you will be fined and possibly have your license removed.

Now going back to licensing sizes, a larger license usually requires at least one year of experience doing home daycare or having an educational background in child development. Usually you will also need to have an assistant. In my own county the maximum number of children went up to fourteen.

Some important factors to remember are that if you have your own children under the age of eleven, you have to include them in your capacity number. If a licensor makes a visit to your new home daycare and you are watching six little ones plus two of your own (all non-school aged), you would be in big trouble. And if all of your ten children are present (including your own), you cannot have any neighbor kids dropping by to play.

Chapter Four

~Your Home-Safety And Preparation~

To obtain a license you will have a fire and home inspection. The fire inspection is usually set up through the county and you they will check to make sure your house is safe. After they check a number of different items (we will go through this later) and approve you, the next step is usually having your licensor make a home inspection. Generally they come in and gives you a list of things that you will need to have corrected in order to get approved. This can take time and several visits. If you are in a hurry to get your license, it is very important to try and childproof your home before the inspection. You will save a lot of time and hassle. Here are some things that are very important when it comes to childproofing your home. Most of them are pretty basic.

Safety Plugs

Every outlet should have a safety plug. Don't forget the bedrooms, under furniture, behind furniture, and even the bathrooms. Get on your hands and knees to look for these buggers.

Smoke Detectors

Do you have enough smoke detectors and are the batteries working?

Stairs

You will need some type of fence or barricade so that the young children do not fall down the stairs. Even if you are watching two or three year olds who are capable of using the stairs, they can be pretty uncoordinated. Never leave a stairway open.

Fire Places

They need to be screened in or in a room that isn't available to the children.

Doors

Any door leading out as an exit will need a single action lock to make it easier to get out if there is an emergency.

Fire Extinguishers

You will usually need a larger model (ABC) or commercial grade extinguisher. It should be accessible and you should know how to use it. I keep mine above my refrigerator.

Heaters

No space heaters are allowed. Your home should be adequately heated and safe.

Bodies Of Water

Any body of water should be fenced in or covered (including hot tubs, swimming pools, and even ponds. An outdoor pool should not be directly accessible from any door or window. And if you have a small wading pool for the children, you will be required to have written approval from the parents to let them go in it. The small wading pools are VERY small. You are better off using a sprinkler in the summer for cooling off.

Back Yard

Either you will need a fenced in back yard or you will need to be with the children every second when they are outside. That means not running inside to use the bathroom quickly.

Look closely at your yard. Are there any sharp objects or other dangerous items accessible to the young children? Lock up items that may harm them. Use common sense and you will find a ton of things that could be dangerous.

Another option to keep the children safe is using your patio deck when you can't be with them 100% of the time. One daycare provider felt uneasy about using her backyard so she kept the children on her upper deck whenever they went outside. Check with your county to find out how tall the railings have to be. My railings were almost a foot too short so I couldn't even use the deck for my children.

Pets

Most states require that your pets be vaccinated for rabies and to even keep them away from the kids, just in case. Children can be rough with animals and even the best tempered dog can be prodded and poked too many times. Check with your licensor to find out what the rules are in your state.

Cribs

Make sure the crib that you are using is heavy duty and in perfect condition. Slats should be no more than 2 3/8 inches apart. Some providers prefer to use Portacribs or Pack and Plays.

You will usually need to do monthly crib inspections to make sure that yours is safe.

Plants

Do you know if any of your houseplants are poisonous? It's best to place them in rooms off limit to the children or get rid of them.

Kitchen Items

Are your knives inaccessible to the kids? Do you have safety locks on your lower cupboards and drawers? Are plastic bags locked away? Make sure your poisonous items are also unavailable. Appliances should also be placed out of reach. Keep your counters clean and poisonous free.

Bathroom

Make sure your shampoos, medicines, makeup, and cleaning products are locked away. A child can easily open up a shampoo bottle and taste it. Anything that is poisonous or has alcohol (mouthwash) needs to be cleared. I put locks on my medicine cabinet. Also check to make sure the children aren't able to lock themselves into the bathroom. If you have locks you will be required to keep a key close to get in quickly if needed. Some providers choose to remove the locks all together.

The following page contains a checklist that you can use to help prepare your home. This is a general list and you should carefully read your state's requirements.

Kitchen Area

_____ Fire Extinguisher-minimum of 2A10BC near cooking areas. Know how to use it.

_____ Sharp knives, plastic bags, matches, cleaning products, medicines, alcoholic beverages and other potential toxics inaccessible to children..

_____ Rubbish-are all containers covered or inaccessible to infants and toddlers.

_____ Separate drinking cups for children

_____ Paper towels for cleaning the children-each needs a separate washcloth so paper towels are easiest.

_____ Food Program-Are you offering well balanced meals, snacks, and plenty of water to children? Enrolling in a food program not only helps you with this, but you also get FREE MONEY for groceries.

_____Well water-do you have a copy of a well test done within the last year?

_____ Diapering is done away from the food preparation area. Dirty diapers shall not be disposed of in the kitchen garbage containers!

_____ Pets cages need to be cleaned and away from the kitchen and dining area. Cat's litter box should be inaccessible to the children. Fish tanks can't be cleaned in the kitchen sink.

Bathroom Area

_____ Toxics and hazardous items like medicines, razors, cleaning products, curling irons, and personal care and grooming items like cosmetics and lotions should be inaccessible.

_____ Garbage containers should be covered or put inside of a closet or cabinet.

_____ Water temperature in the sinks and tubs should be less than 120 degress F.

_____ Diapering surface should be smooth and nonabsorbent.

_____ Do you have a covered diaper disposal container lined with disposable plastic bags?

_____ Do you have a bleach-water solution to clean the surface between each diaper change?

_____ Are diapers out of reach to infants and toddlers?

Hand-washing

_____ Do caregivers wash their hands with soap and water and use a single use towel to dry their hands after each change?

_____ Do caregivers wash with soap and water and use a single towel use to dry hands after assisting the children on the toilet?

_____ Wash hands with soap and water and use single-use towel after cleaning diaper changing area, before preparing foods, and after using the bathroom yourself.

_____ Make sure children use a single-use towel after using the potty chair or toilet.

_____ Children need to wash hands with soap before eating a meal or snack.

_____ Children need to wash with soap and water when hands are soiled.

_____ Each child needs a separate towel, wash cloth, drinking cups, combs, and other personal items.

Paper Towels, Paper Towels, Paper Towels!

First Aid Kit

_____ Do you have a first aid kit complete with

_____ bandages

_____ sterile compresses

_____ scissors

_____ instant ice pack

_____ oral or surface thermometer

_____ mild liquid soap

_____ adhesive tape

_____ first aid manual

_____ Is the first aid kit taken with you on field trips?

Bedrooms

_____ Do you have two exits from every room, one of which is a door or window that goes directly outside?

_____ If the exit going directly outside is a window, does it have at least 5.7 square feet of clear opening?

_____ Do you have a smoke detector on each level of your home? It is recommended that you have a smoke detector outside each sleeping area in particular.

_____ Do they all work?

_____ Are all toxic and hazardous items such as medicines, colognes, matches, deodorants, scissors, sewing supplies, personal care and grooming products inaccessible to children?

_____ Do you have a bathroom adjacent to the bedroom that needs to be checked as well?

_____ Is there a firearm and is it in a locked location?

_____ Is the ammunition for the firearm stored in a separate location from the firearm?

Sleeping Space

_____ Do you have a crib or port-a-crib-no mesh sides- for each child under a year old? Cribs must have a waterproof mattress and a rail pattern no more than 2 3/8 inches wide.

_____ Is there a mat, crib, cot, bed, sofa, or sleeping bag for each toddler and preschool child?

_____ Is the equipment safe and sturdy?

_____ Clean bedding for each child?

Children's Play Area

_____ Are outlets capped when not in use?

_____ Extension cords cannot be used on an ongoing basis in place of permanent wiring. When being used temporarily they cannot extend under floor coverings or doorways.

_____ Are all major electrical appliances properly installed and grounded?_____ Are children under school age able to reach scissors, knives, matches, plastic bags, or sharp tools or objects? These must be up high or locked away. Any use of scissors must be supervised.

_____ Are any children in care able to reach toxic paints, perfumes, makeup, medicines, chemicals, detergents, poisonous plants, alcohol, chipped or peeling paint?

_____ Is the environment free from any build-up of dirt or rubbish.

_____ If diapers are changed in this area, is the pad sanitized with a bleach solution after every use and cleaned when soiled?

_____ Is a permanent barrier around any fireplace used during child care?

_____ Are guards in place around space heaters or other hot surfaces?

_____ Is the furnace and hot water heater inaccessible to children?

_____ Are book cases secured firmly to the walls?

_____ No poisonous plants, including oleanders, elephant ears, or lilies of the valley.

Gates

_____ do all stairs leading up or down from the play area have gates or barriers blocking access to them when children between 6 and 18 months old are in care?

Activities

_____Are activities scheduled both indoors and outdoors permitting.

_____Do you have activities you engage in with the children and direct as well as giving them other time to pick an activity themselves?

Outdoor Play

_____Is your deck 30 inches or more above the ground?

_____Does it have a guardrail around it? If it is 30 inches above the ground it needs one. The guardrail must have vertical spindles that are no more than 4 inches apart.

_____If there are three or more steps, do they have a handrail? Are the backs of the steps (the risers) enclosed?

Pets

_____Is the play area free of animal excrement

_____Have parents been notified of the presence of pets?

_____Are children supervised at all times when handling animals?

_____Remember you must notify parents the same day if their child's skin is broken by a pet bite or scratch. An agent of the Board of Health (usually the local police) must be notified of any bite.

Fences

_____Fences are not always required but may be if there are railroad tracks, water, traffic, or heavy machinery adjacent to the property. A worker may need to look at your property in order to know for sure if a fence is needed.

_____Do you have a pond, drainage pond, or swimming pool, or other body of water adjacent to your property?

_____Does the street or road adjacent to your house have a speed limit over 35 miles an hour?

Supervision

_____ when school age children are outside on their own, do you have good sight lines to know what they are up to?

_____ If you are inside with the children under school age and have to respond to older children outside, what will you do with the little children indoors?

_____ How easily can you respond to older children given your home's layout and levels?

_____ When you are outside with all the young children under school age, how do you handle it when you need to take a child indoors to use the bathroom?

Playground Equipment

_____ Is the outdoor play equipment appropriate to the age of the children using it?

_____ Is the outdoor equipment in good repair?

_____ Is the outdoor play equipment free of lead-based paint?

Smoking is prohibited in a child care home during its hours of operation

Nursery Safety

More infants die every year in accidents involving cribs than with any other nursery product. Thousand of infants are seriously injured enough to require treatment in hospital emergency rooms.

The CPSC discourages the use of used cribs. Use a crib that meets Federal safety regulations and industry voluntary standards. Make sure it has a tight fitting mattress. Check the labeling on these products to make sure they meet safety requirements.

Check the crib and replace any missing parts such as screws, bolts, or mattress support hangers before placing a child into it. Make sure that all screws and bolts are securely tightened. Any screw inserted into a wood component cannot be tightened securely should be replaced by one that fits. On cribs where the mattress support is suspended by hangers attached to hooks on the end panels, check frequently to be sure they have not become disconnected. Never use a crib with a broken or missing part.

Avoid older cribs with headboard and footboard designs that may allow an infant's head to become caught in the openings between the corner post and the top rail or in the other openings in the top edge of the headboard structure. These openings may lead to strangulation.

Never use a crib with missing slats. If you repair or refinish a crib, use only lead-free enamel paint and let it dry so there is no residual fumes. Check the label to make sure the manufacturer does not recommend against using it on cribs.

To reduce the risk of Sudden Death Syndrome (SIDS) and prevent suffocation, put a baby on his or her back in a crib on a firm flat mattress. Never let a child sleep temporarily in an adult bed or waterbed. Never use a pillow.

Never put a crib near a window blind or drapery. Never use strings to hand any object such as a mobile or toy or diaper bag near the crib.

Never tie a pacifier or teether around a child's neck. Remove bibs and necklaces whenever placed in a crib or playpen.

Never use plastic bags as mattress covers to prevent suffocation.

Secure bumper pads around the entire crib and snap or tie it in place at least in each corner, in the middle of each long side, and on both the top and bottom edges. Cut off any excess string length.

Make sure Crib Gyms are installed securely at both ends so they cannot be pulled down. Remove them along with any mobiles when the baby begins to push up on hands and knees.

Mobiles and any other toys that hang over a crib should be out of reach of a child.

A month safety inspection will be required by you for every crib used in daycare. You will be required to check for recalls as well. The online website to check for these recalls (as of 2010) is:

www.cpsc.gov/cgi-bin/prod.aspx

Baby Gates

Baby gates are used at the top and bottom of stairs or in open doorways to prevent toddlers from falling or entering unsafe areas. But some gates themselves are dangerous. The Commission warns parents and others who care for children that an entrapment and strangulation hazard exists with accordion-style baby gates that have large V-shaped openings along the top edge and diamond-shaped openings between the slats. CPSC knows of deaths that occurred when children's heads were entrapped in the V-shaped or diamond-shaped openings when they attempted to crawl through or over the gates. Although these hazardous accordion style baby gates haven't been sold since 1985, you may still find them at yard or garage sales.

If you will be using a baby gate, choose one with a straight top edge and rigid bars or mesh screen, or an accordion-style gate with SMALL V-shapes and diamond shaped openings. Entrances to V-shapes should be no more than 1-1/2 inches in width to prevent head entrapment.

Be sure the baby gate is securely anchored in the doorway or stairway it is blocking. Children have pushed gates over and fallen down stairs.

Gates that are retained with an expanding pressure bar should be installed with this bar on the side away from the child. A pressure bar may be used as a toehold by a child to climb over a gate. Pressure gates are not recommended for the top of a stairway.

Circular wooden enclosures that expand, accordion-style, can present many hazards. The CPSC recommends that you do not use an accordion-style expandable enclosure with V-shaped or diamond-shaped openings.

High Chairs

Each year thousands of children are injured due to high chairs. Most of the injuries result from falls when the restraining straps are not used or when children aren't supervised. The majority of deaths occurred when children slipped down under the tray and then strangled. Most were not restrained or only by a waist belt.

To help prevent injuries use a high chair that has a waist strap and one that runs between the legs. While in the chair the children should ALWAYS be restrained by both straps. Without the two straps the child can stand in the chair and topple from the chair, or slide under the tray and strangle on the waist strap.

Other accidents occur when the chair tips over if an active child pushes off from a table or wall, stands up in the high chair, or rocks it back and forth.

If you are buying a new high chair, select one that has a wide base for stability. Make sure that there is a waste buckle that cannot be fastened unless the crotch strap is used. Consider a chair that has a post between the legs to prevent the child from slipping down.

If using a secondhand chair, check the condition of the straps and their attachments to make sure they work properly.

Hook-On Chairs

These are substitutes for high chairs and are attached to the edge of a table. There have been reports of children falling out of these chairs or dislodging the chair from the table.

Never place the chair where the child's feet can reach the table supports, benches, or chairs, to push off from and dislodge the chair.

Always use restraining straps.

Check the security of the chair when it's clamped down by pulling backwards on the chair.

Never leave a child unattended.

Never use this on a glass top, single pedestal, or unstable table.

Playpens

Deaths have occurred when the drop-sides of mesh playpens and cribs were left in the down position. When a mesh side is left down, the mesh hangs loosely, forming a pocket or gap between the edge of the floor panel and the side. Young infants, even a few weeks old can move to the edge and fall into the loose mesh pocket where they can be trapped and suffocate. New playpens have warning labels that alert parents and others to never leave infants in the playpen with the sides in the down position.

If you are buying a new playpen, look for one that has top rails that automatically lock when lifted into the normal use position. Also look for mesh netting with a very small weave, less than ¼ inches. Slat spaces on a wooden playpen should be no more than 2-3/8 inches in width.

Always remove large toys, bumper pads, or boxes from inside of a playpen, they can be used for climbing out. Never hang toys from the sides with string or cords.

Never use a playpen with holes in the mesh sides. These could entrap a child's head and cause strangulation.

Never use a pad that does not fit snugly and never add a second pad or mattress. Babies have suffocated when trapped between the mattresses or between the side and mattress that was too small.

Never leave a rattle, squeeze toy, teether, or other small object in a crib when the baby is sleeping. Avoid rattles and squeeze toys with ball-shaped ends.

Toy chests

The CPSC has received reports of death and brain damage as a result of toy chest lids falling on children's heads or necks. These include those specifically manufactured for toy storage as well as trunks, wicker chests, wooden storage chests, and other similar items.

Most of the children were under two years of age. Accidents occurred when children were reaching over and into the chest when the lid dropped.

Another fatal but less frequent hazard is suffocation, which resulted in the deaths of several children when they climbed into a toy chest to hide or sleep.

If buying a new toy chest, look for one that has a support that will hold the hinged lid open in any position in which it is placed or buy one with a detached lid or door.

Look for a chest with ventilation holes that will not be blocked if the chest is placed against a wall, or a chest which when closed, has a gap between the lid and the sides of the chest.

Make sure the lid of the toy chest does not have a latch.

Walkers

Walkers are not recommended. It is estimated that more children are injured in baby walkers than with any other nursery product. Accidents happen even when a caregiver is nearby. Almost all of the victims are children under 15 months of age.

USE an activity center instead of a walker to keep your child entertained as well as safe.

Bouncers or Carrier Seats

Most injuries from these items result from falls; infants falling out of carriers or the seat collapses with the infant in it. Deaths have occurred when the seats were placed on beds, sofas, or other soft surfaces, and then tipped over.

Safety Tips

The Carrier should have a wide sturdy base for stability

Stay within an arm's reach when placed on a table, counter, or other piece of furniture.

Always use the safety belts.

Never use a carrier seat as an infant car seat.

Changing Tables

Most injuries associated with changing tables occur when children fall from the changing table to the floor. Look for a table with safety straps and always use them.

Pacifiers

Pacifiers must be strong enough to not separate into small pieces. The shields must be large enough and firm enough to prevent the pacifier from being drawn entirely into the baby's mouth and should have ventilation holes.

Never tie a pacifier around a baby's neck as it presents a strangulation danger.

Strollers

Never leave an infant to sleep when in the backrest reclined position. A child may slip into a leg opening and become entrapped by the head resulting in death.

Always secure the seat belt. Never use a pillow, folded quilt, or blanket as a mattress in a stroller or carriage.

Close the opening between the hand rest (grab bar) and seat when using a stroller in the reclined carriage position.

Chapter Five

~Forms~Contracts~Handbooks~Policies~

A handbook of written policies is very important tool in running a successful daycare. Not only should you have written policies but you should always give a copy to the parents to read before you watch their children. Have them sign them as well so that they will understand your policies and there won't be any conflicts later.

Examples of things to include in your policies would be fees, holidays, sick days, hours, late payments, etc.

Most daycare providers have a probationary period. I chose to give each child a two week trial period. This way if things do not work out, you or the parent have the opportunity to gracefully withdraw from the contract. Sometimes not every child will be happy and comfortable with your daycare, nor will you be happy with every child (or parent!).

FEES

When starting out you want to be competitive with your pricing. If you are charging more than providers who've been in the business for awhile, you will find it difficult to compete. A lot of parents will look at the length of time you've been doing daycare as well as fees when making their decisions.

One way to drum up business is to offer a discount. I myself would take $100 off the third week when business was slow and I needed to find a new child. This usually worked.

Many parents just need part-time daycare. This is very common. Some providers choose to only take full-time children, or charge a full-time rate even for part-time care, especially for infants and toddlers. However if you are great with juggling different hours and are careful to not have too many kids at one time, you could do very well with only part-time kids.

Another important factor is the age of the child. It is more time-consuming to care for an infant or toddler than it is for a preschooler. An infant is usually 6 weeks to 12 months and a toddler is from twelve months to two years. After two years they are considered a preschooler. You can charge more for the younger children, the states allow this but usually with a limit or cap. Check with your county or other providers to see what is acceptable for pricing.

If you offer a curriculum or a unique type of daycare, then most parents will be willing to pay a little extra. For example, you are giving the children piano or dance lessons. Or maybe you are willing to pick up the children from school or have a drop-in policy.

When you've decided what you are going to charge, make sure that you are clear in your contracts as to when payments are expected. Most providers will require payment from the parents on the Monday beginning care. Some will even request it the Friday before care is needed. Whichever you decide, be vigil with it.

Some providers will charge a late payment fee and a bounced check fee. This is a great idea. Make sure to put it into your contract and policy agreement.

Hours of Operation and Late Fees

You will need to decide what hours you will be willing to accept children. In many states during your first year you are only able to watch them around regular business hours (6am-6:00pm). After the first year you may be able to watch children during a second shift or over-night. Check with your licensor for more information.

After you have set your hours, make sure that in your contract you have the parents write in the time-frames that are needed for daycare. You might also want to charge a late fee for parents picking up their children late (after you are closed). If you do not reflect a late payment fee, beware from parents who will be chronically late.

Holiday Schedule

It is usually standard for most childcares to charge for holidays that fall during the week. These days will include New Years Eve and Day, Christmas Eve and Day, Thanksgiving (Thursday and Friday), Veterans Day, Columbus Day, Labor Day, Independence Day, Memorial Day, President's Day, and Martin Luther King JR Day.

Vacations

When a child goes on vacation a parent should pay you something to hold their spot. Most providers charge half the normal fee for care. You should also request at least a month's notice.

If you go on vacation, you will need to decide if you are going to charge the parents. Some providers will charge half the normal fee or nothing at all. Make sure you put this into your policy and handbook.

Termination Policy

There will be times when a contract will be terminated by you or the parent. Since your paycheck will be affected, requiring a two week notice is appropriate.

There are many reasons why a parent or you will remove a child from daycare. Sometimes a parent relocates or there are behavioral problems with the child (and sometimes the parent!). For the better interest of your sanity and the other children's in your care, a termination policy is something good to go over in your handbook.

Here are some other common reasons for terminations:

- A child hurts the other children consistently.

- A child who swears, throws daily tantrums, ignores discipline. Sometimes the child needs therapeutic care.

- A child isn't happy.

- A parent doesn't pay on time or sometimes at all.

- A parent disagrees with the caregivers policies.

- A parent is unable or refuses to acknowledge requests for diapers, warm clothes, etc.

- Abuse of the child-you are required by law to report any suspected abuse and the parent will more than likely pull the child out of your care or be too angry or disruptive for you to keep the child in your care.

Sickness

In this business you will be surrounded by children getting sick. Your job is to *try* to ensure that a sick child doesn't share their illness. Especially with the H1N1 virus.

The CDC recommends the following:

Symptoms of seasonal flu and 2009 H1N1 flu include fever, cough, sore throat, runny or stuffy nose, body aches, headache, chills, and tiredness. Some people may also have vomiting and diarrhea. People may be infected with the flu, including the 2009 H1N1 flu and have respiratory symptoms without a fever. Sick children and staff should stay at home until at least 24 hours after they no longer have a fever (100 degrees Fahrenheit or 37.8 degrees Celsius measured by mouth) or signs and symptoms of a fever (has chills, feels very warm to the touch, has a flushed appearance, or is sweating) without the use of fever-reducing medicine.

Some providers will ask parents to keep children home during the first couple of days of a bad cold or cough. Also if a child is contagious, running a fever over 101 degrees, is throwing up, or has any other severe symptoms, you should call the parents and have the child sent home.

If you have to administer medicine to a sick child, you will need a written consent form from the parent.

If you get sick, you should try to have a person lined up who can substitute for you. It is good to meet with other providers in your area who may be able to substitute, or use your spouse if available. Check with your state to see what classes are needed for a substitute. This person will have had a background check as well, so normally it is someone in your home or another professional caregiver.

Meals

You will be responsible for providing nutritious meals and snacks for the children when they are in your care. By providing food for the children you are eligible for reimbursement from CACFP (Child and Adult Care Food Program). The CACFP provides reimbursement for meals and snacks served to small groups of children receiving nonresidential day care in private homes that are licensed, registered, or approved to provide family child care. Check with this website for more information or your licensor.

www.fns.usda.gov/cnd/care/Homes

Let me tell you, these food programs are **wonderful**. You are required to do some paperwork for the reimbursements, but I can't stress enough how great it is. Free money people! It's like getting a raise. You will get a monthly check to help pay for your groceries. It's easy and parents love to know their children are getting fed nutritiously.

Discipline Policies

It is your job to set limits and to keep the children safe. A written policy is a great way to let your parents know what to expect when rules are broken. Whether it is time outs or taking a toy away from a child who is misbehaving, it is important to set rules and stick with them. And of course you are not allowed to spank or cause any type of physical discomfort to a child. Nor are you allowed to hold back snacks or food. Children misbehave and they learn from discussion, not from physical abuse. It is illogical to hit a child for hitting another.

Time outs are a great took for discipline. I used a separate chair for the time out spot and a child would have to sit down for the length of minutes of their age. A four year old would sit for four minutes, a three year old for three, etc. Then we would discuss what they did wrong and I would have them repeat it to make sure they were listening.

If you have a child who is constantly misbehaving and it is too much for you, terminate the contract. Some children need extra special care and you may not be able to provide it. Especially if they are constantly taking your time away from the other children or treating the other children badly.

Potty Training

Potty training can be a lot of work. You are responsible for assisting with this and it usually occurs between twenty and thirty six months. Make sure that the parent sends extra clothing during this process and even pull-ups for nap-time. Children are different and one child may catch on right away, and others have accidents even at four or five years old. I had children who were still having accidents at seven years old. Patience and extra clothing are a necessity.

Other Policies

As time goes by you will incorporate many other policies that fit specifically with your daycare. Whether it's about transporting children or impairment policies (a parent arrives under the influence of something), it is a good idea to be very detailed so there are no questions later.

Creating your Policy Handbook and Contracts

There are many resources and examples on the internet of handbooks and contracts. I have included examples at the end of the book as well.

When interviewing parents and children for daycare, you will usually get a sense of whether or not they are thinking about signing up. If they ask you a lot of questions and seem excited about your child care, then it's a great sign. The ones that do not and state they have "just begun looking' are usually never seen from again.

When I first started, I gave everyone that walked in the door a copy of my handbook, policies, food program information, forms the state required, I mean *everything*. As time went by I found that I wasted a lot of paper and would only give out my policy handbook, unless they wanted to give me a deposit on the spot. You will get frustrated at times and find that parents can be very slow at making decisions when it comes to their children's care. This is very normal and you should expect it. You will be surprised however, at the amount of times a parent will suddenly call you back out of the blue and request enrollment forms. This happened more times than I could count. Just be patient and everything will fall into place.

Chapter Six

~Supplies~

How much does it cost to outfit your daycare? Most providers have very little to begin with and a meager budget. The good news is that here are many resources available to help supply your new business with little out of pocket. You can always start small and add on later as well.

In the summer you can visit garage sales, yard sales, and flea markets for many supplies. In the winter you can visit the second hand stores and even find great deals on Craig's List. I picked up many free items on Craig's List to outfit my daycare. Just be very cautious when you are picking up an item from a stranger and never go alone to pick up an item.

As far as high chairs, playpens and cribs go, remember to check for recalls and make sure they are in good working order.

To operate a family child care program successfully in your home, you will need to obtain some extra furniture and equipment. Here are some essentials for working with young children:

- A child-size table and chairs

- Low shelves to store toys and materials

- Places to nap (cots, mats, cribs, playpen)

- Stroller that accompanies two or even three children

- High chair and booster seats

When you are looking for items make sure that they are well made and sturdy without small detachable pieces. Some good things to consider when purchasing toys:

- They do not have sharp edges, points, splinters

- The items aren't too heavy.

- Riding toys are stable

- All painted toys are labeled nontoxic

- Metal toys aren't rusty.

Toys and Materials for infants:

- Crib Mobile

- Washable and cuddly toys

- Sturdy rattles

- Plastic key rings

- Non-breakable plastic mirror

- Teething rings

- Squeaky toys

- Chime balls

- Toy phones

- Balls of different sizes

- Soft cloth blocks

- Stacking toys

- Nontoxic plastic books

- Household items they can play with such as pots, pans, spatulas, wooden spoons, plastic food containers, coffee cans with lids, measuring cups.

For toddlers:

- Music-compact discs of music or stories

- Push and pull toys

- Peg boards

- Wooden puzzles

- People or animal figure toys

- Doctor's kit

- Trucks, cars, wagons

- Large crayons

- Pails and shovels

- Wagons and riding toys

- Books (you can get from the public library)

- Household items to play with such as sieves, funnels, strainers, mixing cups, sponges, and spoons.

For preschoolers:

- Play house or farm sets with figures

- Plastic snapping blocks

- Games

- Interlocking toys

- Magnetic Boards

- Wooden or sturdy cardboard puzzles

- Crayons and washable markers

- Glue

- Scissors

- Balls

- Hula Hoops

- Wagons

- Tricycles

- Water-based paints and brushes

- Props for playing dramatic play such as brooms, mops, mirrors, plastic dishes, dress up clothes, hats, costume jewelry, fake food, squirt bottles, combs, rakes, etc

- Art materials such as feathers, glitter, wrapping paper, paper towel tubes, pipe cleaners.

For School Agers

- Board games

- Decks of cards

- Jigsaw puzzles

- Craft kits such as Origami and Bead Design

- Art materials such as pens, colored pencils, markers, crayons, chalk, paint

- Outdoor equipment such as jump ropes, balls, and various other items.

- Large Cardboard boxes, library books, tapes, sewing materials, flashlights, rulers, etc

To store all of your materials, use low bookcases or plastic milk crates. You can also buy toys shelves pretty inexpensively through the internet (do some research). I purchased mine through Toys R Us.

Chapter Seven

~Your days with the Children~

Daily Schedule

Having a daily schedule is essential for any successful daycare. Not only do the parents like to know what is going on during the day, but young children like routines. This schedule will help them learn the order of the day and will be comforting for them. Here is just one example of a daily schedule:

6:30-8:30 am   Children arrive and breakfast is served. Children are allowed to help with cleaning up breakfast and can play with table toys or read books.

8:30-10:00 am Group Activities such as painting, water play, or cooking. Babies wake up from early nap or placed down for one.

10:00-10:30 am Snack time

10:30-11:15 am Outside Activities

11:15-12:00 pm Free Play

12:00-1:00 pm Lunch and then cleanup

1:00-1:15 pm Story Time

1:15-3:15 pm Rest Period

3:15-3:45 pm Snack-time for everyone including school aged children.

3:45-4:30 pm Active indoor or outdoor play.

4:30-5:00 pm Quiet Group Activity

5:00-6:00 pm Children color or play with table toys until parents arrive.

*Please note that during the rest period, preschool children who can't sleep can play quietly on their cots or look at books.

Rest Periods or Quiet Time can be challenging when you have children of different age groups. Here are some suggestions for making it a relaxing period for everyone:

- Have each child sleep in the same cot, bed, or crib every day.

- Encourage children to bring favorite sleep toys or blankets from home.

- Plan a quiet activity right before rest time, such as a story or soft music.

- Give children time to settle down at their own pace. They shouldn't be forced to sleep but encouraged to relax.

Meal and Snack Times

Meals are a very important part of your day. They have to be nutritious and not from a can. Fortunately your local food program will help you with menu and food ideas. They will also give you information on how much food the children should eat and out of which food groups.

Your snacks and meals can be simple and easy to prepare. Many can even be prepared the day before.

On the next few pages are some great food ideas. A good idea is to plan your meals a week in advance. You can then create a menu and send them home with the children's parents so that they can see what you are serving their children.

BREAKFAST IDEAS

milk	milk	milk
banana	peaches	grapefruit
whole wheat biscuits	blueberry muffins	cinnamon toast
milk	milk	milk
orange juice	grapefruit	fruit cup
bran muffins	rice krispies	pancakes
milk	milk	milk
bananas	apricot halves	pears
oatmeal	toast	waffles
milk	milk	milk
banana	orange juice	grape juice
cornflakes	bagel	English muffin
milk	milk	milk
watermelon	banana	peaches
corn muffins	wheat chex	cherrios
milk	milk	milk
fruit cocktail	tomato juice	green grapes
rye toast	grilled cheese sand.	cream of wheat
cheese		
milk	milk	milk
watermelon	prunes	potato pancakes
banana bread	muffins	toast
scrambled egg	sausage	
milk	milk	milk
grape juice	grape juice	peaches
french toast sticks	cream of wheat	shredded wheat
milk	milk	milk
pineapple juice	hash browns	plum
wheat toast	malt-o-meal	apple muffins

Lunch Ideas

milk	milk	milk
roast beef sand	Steak Nuggets	ground turkey
baked beans	cole slaw	broccoli
coleslaw	fruit kabobs	peaches
bun	breading	macaroni
milk	milk	milk
ham	meat loaf	mushroom omelet
scalloped potatoes	baked potato	hashbrowns
spinach	beets	mixed fruit
roll	blueberry muffin	English muffins
milk	milk	milk
chicken nuggets	corn dog	cheese omelet
french fries	potatoes	carrots mixed
fruit	tossed salad	green grapes
breading	breading	roll
milk	milk	milk
baked turkey leg	pork chops	ham & beans
peas	green beans	carrot sticks
cranberry sauce (whole)	french fries	apple wedges
toast	apple-orange bread	cornbread
milk	milk	milk
beef stew (HM)	liver & onions	tuna sandwich
carrots/potatoes	baked potatoes	carrot/celery
applesauce	fruit cocktail	oranges
roll	blueberry muffin	bread
milk	milk	milk
mac & cheese	turkey joes	fish sticks
peas/carrots	broccoli	french fries
cantalope	pears	cherries
macaroni	bun	bread
milk	milk	milk
beef & noodles	chicken veg. soup	tuna/noodle
carrots	potatoes	melon
applesauce	peaches	celery

noodles	crackers/cheese	noodle
milk	milk	milk
egg salad sand	chicken & noodles	sausage pizza
potato wedges	peas	tossed salad
plums	grapes	watermelon
whole wheat	bread noodles	crust
milk	milk	milk
creamed chicken	hamb. sauc	baked fish
peas	tossed salad	baked squash
strawberries	fruit cocktail	fruit cup
biscuits	spaghetti	bread
milk	milk	milk
beef burrito	hamburgers	egg sandwich
pinto beans	coleslaw	tomato slices
bananas in jello	apple wedges	apple wedges
tortilla bun bread		

SNACK IDEAS

ginger bread	rice pudding	rice cakes
applesauce	milk	milk
peanut butter balls	toasted bagel	bran muffin
milk	apple juice	pineapple juice
fruit yogurt	whole wheat toast	deviled egg
vanilla wafers	peanut butter	milk
soft pretzel	oatmeal cookies	vegetable sticks
pear-grape juice	milk	cot. cheese dip
fruit & cheese kabobs	pocket bread	English muffin
orange juice	tuna filling	melted cheese
bread stick	apple wedges	apple muffin
pine/orange juice	peanut butter	milk
tortilla	cocoa (with milk)	cereal snack bar
mix bean dip	animal crackers	milk

Remember that many children are fussy eaters. This can be corrected. Chances are if they see other children eating the foods they thought they would dislike, they will try it and will eventually enjoy it. One great way that I got my children to try new foods was to have them assist me with the preparation. Children love helping out in the kitchen.

Never force a child to eat something or punish him or her for not finishing everything on their plate.

If you are not much of a cook, don't be discouraged. There are many simple meals that you can make for the children and lots of resources on the internet. The most important thing is to sign up with a Government Food program. They will come to your home and guide you through everything. There is no cost to you and you will get free money for your food. It's well worth it.

Quiet Time

At my house we have *Quiet Time*. This is basically nap or rest time during the day. Believe me they will need this and so will you.

Playing soft classical music or lullabies are a great way to begin quiet time. Not only does it relax the children, but they learn to recognize different songs.

Infants nap frequently and so quiet time is very different for them. But for the children aged two and up, we take out our cots every day at the same time and they are required to rest. With one and two year olds it can be very challenging. Most of the time, I end up putting them in a crib or playpen for their naps. They are generally too restless and want to get up and play with toys.

Older children that are four and five are allowed to lie in their cots and quietly read books or work on homework (if they are in kindergarten).

Free Play- Outside

Being outdoors is not only a great opportunity to use up some of their endless energy, but it is also important for a child's health. Fresh air and Vitamin E is a necessity for growth and development.

The outdoors extends a child's world and provides new areas for play and exploration. As they play tag, hide and seek, and hopscotch, they are learning and refining their motor skills.

Other senses are also learning new things. They can touch and smell flowers. Run through a sprinkler and giggle in surprise when they get wet. Watch as plants grow and birds lay their eggs.

Children develop physically and emotionally outdoors. Playing a game with other children, learning to jump, coordinating eye and hand movements (chalk) and refining small muscle skills (playing in the sand).

There are many things that you can do outdoors with the children. Here is a list of different ideas to keep them busy.

- Digging and pouring-buckets and shovels, funnels, plastic bowls, spoons, sifters, cars trucks, pots, pans, boxes.

- Sand and water play-You can use sandboxes, wading pools, plastic dish tubs, even an old tire as a sandbox frame.

- Planting a garden-use child-sized garden tools or sturdy wooden or plastic spoons, seeds or plants, dirt, fertilizer, watering cans, measuring cups.

- Water Play-Small wading pool, sprinkler, garden hose, watering can, paint brushes and buckets (paint the house).

- Games-Hide and Seek, Follow the Leader, Leap Frog, Jump Rope, Bean Bag Toss.

- Picnics- out of the sun.

- Outdoor Dramatic Play- a large box to create a playhouse, blankets, tablecloths, rope, plastic riding toys, wheelbarrows. Children can create a pretend world and have a lot of fun.

- Walks are a wonderful way to explore the outdoor environment. Take the children out for a walk and then have them draw pictures of what they encountered.

Indoor Activities and Free Play

We went over some of the toys to outfit your daycare in a previous chapter. If you have the room you can designate different corners of your daycare for different types of fun. In one space you could keep the dolls and dramatic play props for them, in another you can have a construction area. Some providers will even have a reading area or nook with large pillows.

Toys are natural learning tools. The problem is that children do get tired of the same toys over time. One thing that you can do is to rotate the different toys so that they don't have the opportunity to play with them every day. You can also change your room around every so often. The children often find this alluring.

Structured time is also a very important tool to use for your daycare. This means that you choose the activity and direct it. Examples of this include Circle Time, Reading Time, Curriculum, Arts and Crafts, and even field trips.

Circle Time is generally done early in the day and is a nice way to start the day. You can sing songs, read books, or share different things.

Reading Time is very important. Books play a major role in helping children grow up to be good readers. By sharing books with children you can set the stage for great reading habits. It also can sooth an upset child, make one laugh, and even excite their imagination.

Curriculums are structured activities that are usually based on different themes. Each month you can assign a different theme and do many different activities relating to it. For example in November you can base your activities around pilgrims, giving thanks, trees, leaves, and even farm animals.

In the next few pages I have listed some activities to show you examples of things that you can do, both indoors and outdoors relating to a curriculum. There is also a ton of information on the internet which will give you even better ideas.

Curriculum Examples

Spring

Delightful Kites

Materials: 9 in. X 12 in. Art Paper, scraps of art paper in assorted colors, scissors and paste, pencil and eraser, ruler, crepe paper strips

Fold and cut out kite shape. Use various colors of paper scraps to create spring kite designs. (flowers, butterflies, birds, etc) Use crepe paper for tails.

Egg Carton Nursery

Materials: Egg carton, 12 half eggshells, potting soil, marigold seeds, teaspoon, water. Procedure: Let your children fill an egg carton with empty halves of egg shells. Have them fill each shell with potting soil and carefully plant one or two marigold seeds in each shell. Water each shell with a teaspoon of water. Seeds will sprout more quickly if the lid of the egg carton is kept closed so that the seeds will stay warm. When the seeds sprout, have the children replant the seedlings outside, crushing each shell as they place it into the ground.

Flower Printing

Materials: Paper, Liquid tempera, Flowers (fresh), Shallow pans (pie tin or cake pan)
Procedure:
1. Give each child a piece of paper.
2. Make three or four different colors of paint. Put into shallow pans.
3. Let child gently dip a flower into paint.
4. Blot flower on paper. Gently.
5. Repeat and repeat to see the light effect.

Hand Print Flowers

You will need: a paper plate for each child, green construction paper, hand shape traced on paper, glue and paint.

Have the children trace their hands on paper about 5 - 7 times. Cut out and paint color of choice. Paint the paper plate (it becomes centre of flower). Cut stem and leaves from green construction paper.

Have the children glue dry painted hands to outside of paper plate (these become petals). Then glue stem and leaves. Let flower dry completely and then display. These flowers make a welcomed addition to any room.

Summer

Watermelon

Have a watermelon party at snack time on a hot June day and save the seeds. Soak them in soapy water, rinse well, and set out to dry on paper towels overnight. From construction paper, cut 3 half-oval shapes for each child: a large one from green, a medium one from white, and a small one from pink or red. Have the children line up the straight edges and glue the paper together to form a slice of watermelon. Use a squeeze bottle of white or clear glue to dot glue all over the pink or red paper, and then place a dried watermelon seed on each dot of glue.

Paper Plate Sun Flowers

Materials: Paper plates, yellow paint, brushes, glue, sunflower seeds, green paper

Activity: Have the children paint their paper plates yellow to make 'flowers'. When plate is dry put glue on plate and glue sunflower seeds on the middle of their plates. Attach them to green paper stems to create a sunflower garden.

Ice Cream in a Bag

Ingredients: 1/2 cup milk, 1 tbsp sugar, 3/4 tbsp vanilla, ice, 6 tbsp salt, 1 large freezer bag, 1 small freezer bag

Put milk, sugar and vanilla into the small bag. Close the bag. Put the ice into the large bag until the bag is half full. Add the salt to the ice. Put the small bag into the large bag, and seal the large bag. Shake the bags for five minutes. Put in freezer for a few minutes until thick like ice cream.

Egg Carton Collections

Give each child an egg carton before going on a nature walk. Encourage the children to put treasures they find along the way in their cartons. When you return from your walk, have the children talk about their treasures. Then let them glue their items on pieces of construction paper

Fall

Window Painting

Paint a fall scene on your window. Use the following recipe and the paint is easily removed. Give each child a window to decorate.

Window Paint
2 Tbsp powdered tempera paint
1 Tbsp warm water
1 tsp Joy dish washing liquid

Measure powdered paint into a container. Mix in water thoroughly to achieve a smooth paste. Add JOY, mixing completely, but gently, to avoid making paint too sudsy. Dries on windows in 5 - 10 minutes and washes off easily with a solution of water and vinegar.

Aluminum Foil Leaves

Pieces of aluminum foil, leaves, glue, construction paper.

Set out pieces of aluminum foil and a variety of fall leaves. Let each child select a leaf, place it under a piece of foil and gently press and rub the foil with his or her hand to get a leaf print. Then have the children glue their leaf prints to the construction paper. This is a great art project but it also can be a science project. They can see the veins and stems and this can start a really great discussion.

Leaf Bracelets

Wrap a piece of masking tape (sticky side out) around each child's wrist.
Go on a nature walk and have children collect one leaf from each of several trees, sticking it on their leaf bracelet.
When the class returns, sit in circle. Teacher holds up each leaf shape in turn and lets children identify similar leaf on their bracelets.
Let children wear their bracelets home and check the types of leaves in their yards.

Leaf Prints

Materials: Liquid tempera, Brushes, Fresh leaves, Paper, Brayers (Available at art supply stores)
Procedure:
1. Paint the back of the leaves with tempera (not too much.)
2. Place paper on top of the leaves (paint side up.)
3. Use a brayer to roll over paper.
4. Lift and see leaf print. \

Winter

Title: *Color Snow*

Materials: Food color, Water, Spray bottles
Fill empty plastic squeeze bottles with water and different colors of food coloring. Let the children squirt the colors onto the snow. Watch the excitement as the snow becomes a rainbow of colors. The next day, examine the snow to observe the melting process.

Snow Gauge

Help your children make a snow gauge.
Materials a large empty coffee can, ruler, marking pen (permanent ink).
1. Place the ruler inside the can. Now mark and number the inches inside of the can.
2. When it snows, place the can outside in a clear place.
3. When it stops snowing, you and your children can tell how deep the snow is by noting which inch mark it has reached.

Snow Tracks

Encourage your children to be snow detectives by looking for tracks in the snow and trying to identify who made the tracks. Examples:
dog tracks
cat tracks
people tracks
bird tracks
other animal tracks

Snowballs

Bring three snowballs inside. Put them in different locations: the refrigerator, the freezer and on a table. Predict how long the snow will last in each place, and check the results.

Story Time

Reading to the children should be a regular part of the day. You can collect books from garage sales, low priced book stores, and the library. I preferred the library for the older children so that we could explore new ones every day. For babies and toddlers, they usually want you to read the same books over and so I would purchase those. Make sure you get plenty of books that are plastic or board books with nontoxic materials.

You should also provide a variety of books, both fiction and non-fiction. My eldest daughter has always been fascinated with dogs so we would read about the different breeds every week.

Television Time

Many providers do not allow TV viewing. Some allow educational shows such as Sesame Street, Barney, and Dora the Explorer. My policy was to allow children to take turns bringing an educational video on Fridays, for movie day.

You will run into parents who do not care if their child watches a movie or two during the day and others who prefer no videos or television at all. Make sure to schedule plenty of fun activities during the day and they will not even miss the television at all. You may want to not have one in the room so that it is forgotten all together.

Birthdays and Holidays

Birthdays are very exciting for children. I usually make a cake or cupcakes to celebrate their special day and then send a special gift home with them; making sure they didn't open it until after they got home.

You might choose to have party favors and decorate as well as having cake and ice cream. The important thing is too treat every child the same when it comes to birthdays.

I love the holidays and of course children do too. Because you will be getting many children from different backgrounds and beliefs, it is important to talk with the parents regarding their own traditions. If they are Jewish, instead of celebrating just

Christmas, you can incorporate the celebration of Hanukkah as well. For Easter you can focus on the egg hunt or the bunny rabbits. Just be sensitive to every family you care for.

Field Trips

If you have a mix of children with different ages, it might be very hard to schedule field trips. If you do it is important to have assistants to help, otherwise you will run into a lot of problems.

When planning field trips, make sure that you have completed the training required for car seat restraints. And make sure that you have signed approval from the parents authorizing you too take them on excursions.

Where to take the children? There are plenty of great options available.

- Zoo
- Park
- Library
- Nature Preserve
- Circus
- Airport
- Train station
- Aquarium
- The Mall
- A carnival
- Roller skating
- Sledding
- A picnic

Chapter Eight

~Teaching and working with children~

You are a going to be responsible for helping the children develop both physically and emotionally. They will look to your for guidance and support as they learn different activities and develop their communication skills.

During the toddler and preschool years, you will notice there is an enormous amount of leaps that occur as they develop. Toddlers focus on today and usually speak with two or three word sentences. As they get closer to age three and four, they begin to comprehend what happened yesterday or what is happening tomorrow. Their sentences will develop very quickly and you will be amazed at the changes.

Infants

Babies love watching you talk and sing. Your voice will comfort them. Sing or hum to them popular songs such as "Twinkle Twinkle Little Star", "BINGO" or "The Itzy Bitzy Spider". I personally love "Head, Shoulders, Knees, and Toes" because it is a catchy tune and it teaches them the parts of their body.

Infants explore toys by using their senses. As they play and watch others, they grow and develop in many ways. To help them grow cognitively, make sure you have stacking toys, blocks, mobiles, squeezing toys, and musical toys. For physical growth, place toys out of reach so that they will attempt to crawl or reach for it. When they are really small, tummy time is essential.

Another great way to teach infants is to talk to them constantly and always describe what you are doing. Try to avoid *baby talk*. When you are feeding them, describe the food and what color it is. If you are rolling a ball to them, talk about the color and size. They pay a lot of attention to your words and understand more than you know.

The most effective way to guide an infant's behavior is to love and respond to their needs. Make sure they do not hurt themselves, change their diapers frequently, feed them when they are hungry and hold them when they need comforting. And of course, never shake or handle a baby roughly. If you get upset, place a baby safely in a crib and take breath. Call someone if you are scared that you can't control your actions.

Toddlers

Toddlers want to do everything by themselves. They tend to get frustrated quite a bit at this stage and you will find them testing your patience constantly. Not only do they have a hard time sharing, they are trying so very hard to communicate the things that they want. As their language begins to develop and they are able to express themselves easier, you should see fewer tantrums. Also to make things easier, provide duplicate toys and when you do see them sharing, reinforce their behavior.

For cognitive development, have toys that they can use independently. Activity centers, shape sorting, activity centers, puzzles, matching games. For physical growth provide riding toys hula hoops, balls, plastic bats (t-ball), and other similar items.

Toddlers are busy little children but most of them will sit still while you read to them. They also love finger painting, coloring, art projects, and especially playdoh. They also love climbing on everything, so make sure that keep a safe environment to prevent accidents

When disciplining toddlers, make sure that you us a calm but firm tone when dealing with their behavior. They learn from example and if you yell at them, they will express their own feelings the same way. Biting, pushing, and slapping are very common for this stage, especially when they are over-tired. I've found that a great way to deal with these situations is to be firm and to explain why their behavior is wrong. If they are hitting other children, move them away from the other child and explain that it's not nice to hit others. Then get them busy doing something else or give them a nap if they are just tired and that is what's needed. My own child went through a stage of biting. She would try to bite anyone that made her very angry. One day when she tried biting me, I placed her fingers into her own mouth and she bit down. It was a total surprise for her. She never tried biting me again and very soon stopped all together.

.

Preschool Children

Children at this stage love playing Hide and Seek, creating forts, and pretend games. They will spend hours playing *house, store, office, doctor, school, etc.* Dramatic play is very important for their development, so make sure that you have things on hand for them to use such as old hats, purses, shoes, costumes, empty boxes and discarded food packages. You don't have to spend a ton of money either, just visit the garage sales and second hand thrift stores.

Preschool children also loved to be read, draw, paint and make crafts. Make sure that you keep supplies on hand so that they never fun out of anything fun to do.

When caring for preschool children, it is important to do a lot of talking and explaining to help teach them about self-discipline. Most children at this age are able to understand the differences between what is unacceptable and acceptable. But they become overwhelmed and misbehave when their judgment gets clouded by their desires. What I have found that works is to try to come up with solutions that is acceptable to them or have them help to solve the problem. If they do not want to share a toy that they brought with on a certain day, ask them where we should store it until they leave. I also had a rule list and we worked on it together, such as no hitting, no pushing, sharing, listening to others, etc. We hung the list up and when a child began to misbehave, we talked about the rules and what they meant. This helped a lot and the children loved coming to me with new rules they thought made sense.

School-Age Children

When trying to find activities for school aged children, look for books, board games, fun science projects, painting pictures and figurines, other art, crafts, and puzzles. Try to find things that stimulate their brains. One fun thing that they like to do is create their own games. You can help them do this by providing cardboard, markers, magazines, and stickers. They also like puzzles and word games.

One thing that my older children always like doing was taking small boxes and building homes for their favorite action figure or stuffed animals. They will spend hours decorating them. Look for shoe boxes, cereal boxes, and cartons.

School aged children can play more independently although they still *crave* praise from adults. They can also be very competitive with each other and there will be many times that you will have to help them find solutions for getting along. Around eight and nine they become more interested in rules and will notice who is getting treated differently, so be cautious and fair.

Music

Make sure to incorporate music in your daycare. Children love music and it's an important part of their development. By giving the children different types of music to listen to and different types instruments and props to experiment, you will support their growth and development.

Some things that you can do to encourage a love for music and movement, is to play favorite children's songs throughout the day. You can even play something quiet and relaxing during nap time.

If you do not have the money to buy musical instruments, you can make your own. Use an empty coffee can with its lid or even an ice cream bucket to make drums. Fill small ice cream containers (Ben and Jerry's) or yogurt containers with bean and seal them with duct tape for homemade Morroccas.

Dancing and movements can be included in music experiences for everyone. Really young children enjoy movements like "Pat-A-Cake" and "Itzy Bitzy Spider". Try dancing with the babies while holding them in your arms. When they begin to stand you can hold their hands and move to the music. When they can walk well, you can play "Ring around the Rosy". And as they get older still you can do the "Hokey Pokey" or even the "Bunny Hop".

Chapter Nine

~Generating Business~

After you have prepared your home, had all of your inspections, and have received your license, the next step is signing up kids. But, before finding the children that you will be caring for, it's important to think about what age groups you are willing to watch.

Infant care is in high demand, but they are a lot more work. The same is with toddlers, although they can play more independently. In my opinion preschool children are the easiest to watch, and some providers only go with that. If you do plan on mixing the children, remember that infants require a lot of attention so providing a curriculum will be very challenging.

When you've decided the age group, check with providers in your area to find out how much they are charging. You can look through Craig's List to inquire, check with your county or licensor to find out what is the range, or go through the phone book and call.

Next, sign up with your local child-care resource and referral center or agency. These agencies can refer parents to you. You can also call the NACCRRA (The National Association of Child Care Resources) or check their website at www.nnaccrra.org.

Other great ways to market your daycare:

- Make flyers and post them at your local libraries, supermarkets, coffee shops, community centers, gymnastic facilities, schools, and churches. You can also distribute them around your neighborhoods.
- Make signs and place them around your neighborhood.
- Advertise on Craigslist. (This is the best business generator I've found)
- Advertise in your local community paper
- Word of mouth-call other daycare providers and introduce yourself. Let them know you are available if they have to turn parents away.
- Creating a website or blog for your daycare.

When preparing flyers for your daycare, you can save money by making your own using a word processing program on your computer. If you are using a business name, you will need to file a business name with your city or county. This is usually a small fee but it sounds more professional.

Kris's Kidz Child Care

Licensed Child Care.

I offer a warm and loving family daycare that is completely designed for your little ones.

No registration fees
Convenient Hours - 7am-6:00pm
Affordable Rates
Preschool Curriculum
Circle Time, Coloring, Music, Science, Group Activities
A safe, learning and nurturing environment
Nutritious Federal Food Program-Breakfast, Lunch, and Snacks
Certified in CPR, First Aid,SIDS, Shaken Baby, and Vehicle Car Restraints
Quiet Neighborhood with fenced in yard
Otter Lake Elementary School Bus-line
*located at 123 Fake Street
Minneapolis, MN 55430

Call Now!

Owner : Kris Middleton
Phone Number: 651-111-1111

Creating a website or blog can be baffling if you are not sure what you are doing. Fortunately you can create a free blog through many resources on the web. I personally like blogger.com through Google. It is pretty easy to manage and they have a great "how to" section.

If you have chosen a name for your business, you may want to purchase a domain name and set up a website. I did this right away and potential customers were able to go directly to my website and fill out a form which would get emailed directly to me. My personal daycare website is www.care4kidzchildcare.com. I've had a lot of great feedback from parents.

Once you've attracted potential customers, you will be scheduling interviews with them. Make sure you have a list of questions for them so that you can screen for potential problems. Some parents may be looking for new care because of children having behavioral problems or even late payments. Here are some great questions to ask:

- Child's name, age, how many need care?
- What hours do they need care for? Explain that your hours are set and ask them if your schedule may conflict with their work schedule.
- Where was the child last placed in care?
- Why do they need knew care?
- Does your child have any special needs I should be aware of?

Finally, when you have done your interviews and found children, make sure the parents place a deposit to hold the spot. Some parents take weeks to figure out where they want to place their children. Many times I had parents who didn't leave deposits and then when I thought I'd never hear from them again, they would call me. When they leave a deposit you can also purchase items needed, baby formula, wet wipes, cereal, etc. The deposit can be applied towards their first week of care.

When your parents have expressed an interest in placing their children with you, make sure you have them give you a deposit to hold their child's spot. This is important because you have limited spots to fill and you need parents who are serious customers. You can also purchase supplies for their child, such as formula or a resting cot.

Besides getting a deposit to hold the spot, you will also need certain forms filled out before you can watch their child. Your licensor will go over these with you. They include immunization forms, food program forms, and state forms.

Chapter Ten

~Managing your business~

Filing and storing accurate records is a must when you own a home daycare. You will need to keep information and copies of paperwork for the state, for the food program, and for your own records. Setting up a home office is also an important part of your business.

I do not have a separate office and my space is limited. I use a lap top and have a large filing case. This works for me. Now if you have the room and can fit a small desk with your printer and filing cabinet, then you are in pretty good shape. The important thing to remember is to know where everything is, and keep accurate records. And talk with your tax specialist, because I am no expert.

Taxes

Now that you own your own business, you will need to keep record of all of your income and expenses for tax time. You will need complete and accurate records in order to file your tax returns. This includes the income from your food program as well.

It is important to keep your business and personal records as separate as you can. Here are some tips for keeping things separate.

- Open up a separate checking account. Deposit all of your business income into this account and use it to pay for just your daycare food and supplies. When you need money write yourself a check from this account to your family account.
- Keep all of your bank statements for both accounts.
- Get a credit card for just your business expenses.
- Contact a tax specialist with questions and to help you file your taxes.

Make sure that you document every payment received from the parents. Not only will you need this for your taxes, but your parents will want you to fill out an IRS form w-10. I also give them an invoice showing how much they paid me. This is important because you want your figures to match the parents. If they do, not you will run into a possible audit from the IRS.

You will also have to provide documents of all your expenses. There are three kinds, direct business, indirect, and capital expenditures.

A direct business expense: is an "ordinary and necessary" cost of running your business. These expenses include Advertising, Car and truck expenses, bad debts, employee benefits, insurance, mortgage interest, legal and professional services, office expenses, renting, leasing, repairs to your home, cleaning supplies, taxes, licenses, travel, meals, entertainment, activity expenses, yard supplies, wages for employees, and food expenses.

There are actually six different ways of calculating your food expenses, which your tax advisor can go over with you. I personally like the three listed below. These are the most widely used.

1. Average cost per serving- take five typical menus for each meal you serve, using menu items from different seasons of the year. Figure the cost of serving these menus to the children in your care. Calculate an average cost per serving per child. You can also use your Tier pricing method from the food program as your average cost per serving as it will be very close.

    Count the number of meals that you served in the year. If you are on the food program, use the meal counts from your monthly claim form. Remember to add to this the total of all non-reimbursed meals and snacks (the food program usually only reimburses two meals and one snack or two snacks and one meal). Now if the number of children in your care was the same all year then your calculation should be fairly easy. If not, you will have to count the meals you served by month or week. For example:

    Jan-June

    Breakfast   3 children x 5 meals per week x 52 weeks = 910 breakfasts

    Lunch   5 children x 5 meals per week x 52 weeks = 1430 lunches

    Snack   5 children x 10 snacks per week x 52 weeks = 2860 snacks

Multiply each total by the average cost per serving per year. This would be your estimated business food expense on your schedule C.

Example = Breakfast = 910 x $1.02 (average cost per serving) = $928.20

Lunch = 1430 x $1.91=$2731.30

Snack = 2860 x $.60 = $1716.00

Total = $5375.55 (schedule C claim)

2. Purchase your food separately. You will need to make sure that you do not use any of this food for your family and can show separate receipts for family supplies. You can't buy any food that is used for both personal and business. Everything has to be separate. Ketchup, mustard, eggs, milk. This is the easiest if you do not have a large family or children.
3. Use the standard meal allowance rate to claim food deductions instead of keeping detailed records and food receipts. You don't even have to participate in the food program to use this method. However if you are on the food program and are reimbursed for the Tier 2, you are only allowed the Tier 1 standard allowance. Using the standard meal allowance may give you a lower risk of an audit by the IRS.

Indirect Business expense or "house expenses": are specific costs you have in maintaining your house. Typically you would use a Time-Space Percentage to figure the deduction you may claim. Some of these specific costs include mortgage loan interest and real estate taxes, casualty losses (from events like earthquakes, floods, accidents, vandalism), Insurance on your home, utilities, home repairs and maintenance(what is pertinent to the useful life of your house including painting, window repair, furnace repair,etc)

Capital Expenditures: is the purchase of any one item for your business that will last for more than one year such as a house, sofa, computer, refrigerator, and a new room. It must cost over $100 and you can only deduct one year's worth of wear and tear. But you can do this every year that you own it. This is called depreciation. Some of the items you will be able to depreciate are your home, home improvements, land improvements, personal property such as furniture, major appliances, play equipment, etc, office equipment, start up expenses, and automobile. Consult an accountant or tax preparer for the specifics.

Just a note – Some providers show a loss in the first year or two of their business. This is generally due to a combination of start-up costs and a slow buildup of enrollment. As long as you keep accurate and orderly records, follow IRS instructions, and get professional help with your taxes, chances are you will be fine.

Figuring your Time-Space Percentage

Your Time Space percentage is the most important tax number that you will calculate for your business. It is also called the home office deduction or the business use of the home. It is entered on IRS for 8829. This percentage represents the proportion of your home that is used for business purposes. You will use it to determine how much of your shared business and personal expenses can be deducted as a business expense. These expenses may include casualty losses, mortgage interest, real estate taxes, house insurance, house repairs and maintenance, utilities, house depreciation, personal property improvements, land improvements, and supply costs for household and toys. Speak to your tax preparer for more information.

TIME-SPACE PERCENTAGE FORMULA

TIME (Number of hours your home is used in business in a year *divided by* Total number of hours in a year which is 8760)

MULTIPLIED BY

SPACE (Number of square feet of your home that is used for business *divided by* Total number of square feet in home)

EQUALS Time-Space Percentage.

If a child stays for two hours beyond your normal closing time, you can add those two hours to your work time. If a child stays overnight, you can count all of the extra hours the child was in your home.

Trying to track the hours you spend caring for children can be tedious but you should develop a system to track at least the extra time beyond your normal hours.

- Business Income-payments from parents and food expense reimbursement from the food program. Payments for low-income children that are paid by the government. Grants from local or state organizations. Fees you've received for conducting a workshop for other providers.

- Track attendance and payments. You should always record the name of the child, the date of each payment, the period covered by each payment, amount paid, method of payment, and check number. You can use a notebook or there are a lot of computer programs available for purchase which can make it easier.

- Food expenses-the food eaten by the children in your care is tax deductible, whether or not it is reimbursed by the food program. Except for the part of the food that you serve your family. Get separate receipts for this food if you can. If you have an employee that is caring for the children, their food is also tax deductible.

When reporting and filing your taxes, the main forms you will be completing are the 1040, Schedules C and SE, and form 8829. The other forms deal with documenting and supporting your income and deductions claims.

Always consult a tax preparer or an accountant for correct information on doing your taxes. I am no expert and this chapter just brushed briefly on some of the things that you will probably need on hand when a real certified accountant does your taxes.

Chapter eleven

~Your First Year~

Your first year will be quite a challenge. It will also be a great learning experience. Not only will you decide if this job is really for you, but you will learn what works in your business and what does not

The truth of the matter is that your first year will fly by and you will probably feel like you were on a rollercoaster ride. That is very normal. Once you enter your second and third year, you will find it much easier and will see the signs of your success. In fact, that is when most providers decide to expand their license and reap the benefits of an even higher profit with help from an assistant (or even a spouse).

Setting goals for yourself during the first year is a great way to keep yourself focused and ready for the growth in your future. Some of the goals that I personally set up for my first year included having a curriculum program set up, purchasing better outdoor equipment for the children, taking two extra courses in child development, and turning a profit.

Most successful businesses also have a mission statement. This is the standards in which you want to run your business. You may want to create one for yourself and post it somewhere. I have a mission statement that I am very proud of. It pretty much sums up my personal philosophy on family child care:

I truly believe that each child is unique and very special. My goal is to provide to them a safe and loving home away from home.

Children are our future and working with them can be both challenging and rewarding. As you learn more about providing quality child care, you will understand what an important job that you have. Success is not only measured in profit, but also in the positive influences that you have on a child's life and well being. Nothing can be quite as rewarding as seeing a child you've mentored, grow and develop into a happy and capable kindergartner who is eager to face the world.

I wish you good luck in your new adventures.

Chapter Twelve

Forms and Examples

The following pages are generic forms and contracts for home daycare. You can change them and use them to your preference.

CHILD CARE AGREEMENT

THIS AGREEMENT is entered into as of this _____day of _____YEAR in Location, by and between (Daycare name and Provider name) (hereinafter referred to as "Provider") and _____(hereinafter referred to as "Parent/Guardian").

This Agreement contains the terms agreed upon between Provider and Parent/Guardian for the care of:

Child:_____D.O.B._____

1. **Security/Holding Deposit.** Parent/Guardian agrees to pay security/holding deposit of $_____.

At the termination of the agreement for care all required fees will be deducted from the security/holding deposit. Any remaining amount will be credited towards the last two weeks of care at (Daycare Name).

Security/Holding Deposit Paid [ ] YES [ ] NO

Check#_____ Date_____

2. **Weekly Rate**. The weekly rate will be $_____ and is due and payable each Friday by 5:30pm. If Child is absent from care the normal weekly rate will be due and payable.

3. **Days and Hours**. The parties to this agreement have agreed to the following schedule of care.

[ ] Monday....... Hours _____ to _____

   [ ] Tuesday...... Hours _____ to _____

   [ ] Wednesday... Hours _____ to _____

   [ ] Thursday....... Hours _____ to _____

   [ ] Friday.............Hours _____ to _____

4. **Late Fees**. Parent/Guardian agrees to pay a late fee of $5.00 per fifteen minutes or portion thereof that Child remains in care after the hours listed in Section 3.

If the weekly rate is not paid by 5:30pm each Friday, Parent/Guardian agrees to pay a late fee in the amount of $10.00 per day until the account is current.

All late fees are due and payable immediately.

5. **Provider Vacation**. The parties agree that Provider will be paid for one week vacation each year.

6. **Term**. The Agreement terminates on December 31, _____. Failure to comply with the terms set forth in this Agreement may, at Provider's discretion, result in immediate termination of Child's enrollment and forfeiture of the security deposit.

A two week written notice is required for any party to terminate this Agreement prior to December 31, _____. Weekly fees will be due and payable on each Friday of the two week notice period.

The parties hereto have executed this Agreement as of the date and year first above written.

Daycare Name   By:_____

                        Parent/Guardian

By:_____

  Provider Name   Date:_____

Date:_____

                 By:_____

                        Parent/Guardian

                 Date:_____

Emergency Form

If I cannot be reached to make arrangements for emergency medical care for my child at the time of an illness, accident, or injury, I give my permission for:

_____

to obtain whatever treatment may be deemed necessary for:

_____

    Name of Child   (D.O.B)

Emergency Parental Consent

When there is a medical emergency, or when a child needs immediate medical treatment Provider name and Daycare name will take all reasonable steps to see that the children in her care receive adequate medical care. When appropriate, Provider name and Daycare name will call 911 and the parent(s).

If the parent(s) cannot be reached, Provider name and Daycare name will call the person(s) listed below who are authorized by the parent to give permission for the medical treatment of the child.

Name: _____ Phone: _____

Name: _____ Phone: _____

If the parent(s) and the authorized person(s) cannot be reached, Provider name and Daycare name will call the child's doctor, identified below. If the child must be taken to a hospital, Provider name and Daycare name will take the child to the child's hospital identified below. If, under the circumstances, it is more reasonable to bring the child to another hospital, Provider name and Daycare name will do so. In the situation where the parent(s) and the person(s) authorized to give permission for medical treatment cannot be reached, the parent authorizes the child's doctor to provide the appropriate medical treatment for the child.

Name of Doctor:	Phone Number:
Address:	
Name of Dentist:	Phone Number
Address:	
Name of Hospital/Clinic:	Phone Number:
Address:	

I agree to promptly notify Bobbie of any changes of the above information.

This form is legally binding, so by signing it, you agree that all of the information provided herein is correct. False Information may result in termination of childcare services, forfeiture of childcare retainer, or both.

Father/Guardian's Signature:	Date:
Mother/Guardian's Signature:	Date:
Provider name and Daycare name:	Date:

General Ledger Month:_____ Year:_____

Date	Check#	Advertising	License Fees	Provider Costs	Supplies	Insurance	Equipment	Repairs

Totals

PAYMENT LEDGER
Year_____

	Family	Family	Family	Family	Family	Family
Month	_____	_____	_____	_____	_____	_____
January	$_____	$_____	$_____	$_____	$_____	$_____
February	$_____	$_____	$_____	$_____	$_____	$_____
March	$_____	$_____	$_____	$_____	$_____	$_____
April	$_____	$_____	$_____	$_____	$_____	$_____
May	$_____	$_____	$_____	$_____	$_____	$_____
June	$_____	$_____	$_____	$_____	$_____	$_____
July	$_____	$_____	$_____	$_____	$_____	$_____

August $_____ $_____ $_____ $_____ $_____ $_____

September $_____ $_____ $_____ $_____ $_____ $_____

October $_____ $_____ $_____ $_____ $_____ $_____

November $_____ $_____ $_____ $_____ $_____ $_____

December $_____ $_____ $_____ $_____ $_____ $_____

Yearly totals $_____ $_____ $_____ $_____ $_____ $_____

<u>New Client Phone Interview Log:</u>

Date: ___/___/___
Name: _____
Address:

_____

_____

Referred
By:_____
Home Phone Number: _____
Work Phone Number: _____
Fax: _____
E-mail: _____

Child(ren)'s Names: Ages:

1-

_____

_____

2-

_____

3-

_____

_____

Parents Hours Worked:

Mother- _____
Father- _____

Hours of care Needed:

From:_____ To:_____

Start Date Needed:

_____

Interview Scheduled? yes_____ no_____ Date_____
Time_____

Materials Mailed or Faxed? yes_____ no_____ Date_____

Record of Incidents and Accident

Name of Child	Date	Time	Incident/Accident

Description of event:

Action taken:

_____

_____

_____

_____

_____

_____

_____

_____

Parent / Guardian Signature:

_____

Provider Signature:

_____

Sample Daily Plan

EARLY MORNING

6:30-8:30 Children arrive and have breakfast if needed. When they are finished they can read books, play quiet games, or do table top activities such as drawing or playdoh.

8:30-9:30 Children can enjoy activities such as finger painting, water play, cooking, or puppet making. As babies wake up, they are brought in to join the group activity. Children help clean up after play time.

9:30-10:30 Outside activities

10:30-11:00 Free Play

LUNCH AND REST

11:00-11:30 Clean-up and story time

11:30-12:00 Lunch Family-style lunch and conversation. After lunch, older children help put food away and clean up. Hands are washed, diapers changed, and teeth brushed.

12:00-1:00 Playtime. Children will assist with picking up before Reading Time

1:00-1:15 Reading Time

1:15-2:30 Everyone (except, perhaps, for a baby who just woke up) has a rest period. Preschool children who can't sleep rest quietly on their mats with a quiet activity such as a book.

AFTERNOON ACTIVITIES

2:30-3:00 Children have a snack together. School-age children arrive and help themselves to a snack. Clean-up follows.

3:00-4:00 Active indoor or outdoor play for all children.

LATE AFTERNOON/EVENING

4:00-4:45 Free play: children play with table toys, blocks, crayons, read books, or build with blocks.

4:45-5:00 Group story time or singing (nondisruptive play for those who don't wish to participate in the group); quiet group activity.

5:00-6:00 Parents Pickup Children. Children remaining can play indoors with books, games, drawing, coloring, etc

TERMINATION NOTICE

Date: _____

Dear Parents: _____

Children's names: _____ and _____.

This note is to inform you that effective _____ childcare services I have been providing to you will be terminated.

Your child's last day of care will be: _____.

Please adhere to termination policies with regards to payment and settling of your account.

Care has been terminated for the following reasons:

_____
_____
_____
_____
_____

If you wish to further discuss your options please contact me at:

_____

During these hours: _____

Received by: _____(Parent or Guardian Signature)

Signed by: _____ (Caregiver Signature)

PERMISSION TO TRANSPORT AND FIELDTRIPS!

I HEREBY GRANT MY CHILD CARE

PROVIDER_____AND EMPLOYEE'S TO TRANSPORT MY CHILD IN LICENSED INSURED VEHICLES, USING FEDERAL APPROVED CHILD SAFETY SEATS AND BELTS ACCORDING TO FEDERAL LAWS..

I UNDERSTAND THAT MY CHILD IS BEING TRANSPORTED FOR THE FOLLOWING REASON: _____.

IF THIS IS A FIELD TRIP, I UNDERSTAND MY CHILD WILL BE VISITING_____

I UNDERSTAND THAT MY CHILD WILL BE AWAY FROM THE DAYCARE FACILITY FROM THIS TIME_____TO THIS TIME_____.

THE DATE OF THIS TRANSPORT / FIELDTRIP IS

_____

PARENTS SIGNATURE

_____ Date_____

PROVIDER SIGNATURE

_____ Date_____

Parent/Child Handbook

A little bit about myself:
Give a brief introduction or history about you and your family.

Hours of operation:
7:30am- 6:00pm. If you need earlier care, I can be available as early as 7:00 am with advance notification.

Enrollment Procedures:

The following forms must be completed by the first day of care:

1. Contract (Parent/Provider Agreement)
2. Child Information card
3. Copy of medical record (showing shots are updated)
3. Medication Permission Statement (if med. is to be given)
4. Infant Formula & Food Waver (if applicable)

I will not be able hold your child's position until I have received a $100 security deposit. The above forms will be needed by the first day of care for your child. The contract must be signed by each person responsible for the child(ren).

Security/Holding Deposit $100 payable to:Your Name
This is required to hold a place for your child in the daycare. It will be credited towards your first week of service.

Trial Period
The first two weeks are considered a trial period for all of us. If your child isn't happy or doesn't adjust, then we will both have the opportunity to cancel the contract. Every child is different and I want to make sure all of the children are happy and comfortable when they are here.

Termination
I would appreciate at least a two week notice if you will not need daycare services so that I can try to fill your child's spot(s).

<u>Vacation and Absences</u>:
I may take up to two weeks of vacation. I will notify you at least 1 month in advance of the dates of those vacations. 1/2 tuition is still due in order to hold your child's spot for daycare for the first week. If I take a second week, payment will not be required.

When you take your children on a weekly vacation, ½ of the tuition is still required to hold their spot.

<u>My Childcare program will be closed on the following holidays:</u>
Christmas Eve, Christmas Day, New Years Day, Memorial Day, the 4th of July, Labor Day, Thanksgiving Day. Payment is still required for holidays.

<u>Your Vacation</u>

When on a weekly vacation, ½ of your payment is required to hold your child's spot for daycare.

<u>Absence due to Illness in my Family:</u>
Although I will make every attempt to be available each day, there will be occasions when another family member or I are very ill and I am unable to provide service. You will be notified as soon as possible if this occurs. I would strongly suggest that you have some kind of back up childcare lined up for these times. When I must be away for a short time (1-3 hours), backup care will be provided by one of my substitute providers. If I am unable to use one of my substitute providers then it will be necessary for me to close for half day or the full day.

There are a limited number of spaces available therefore weekly payments are not based on a child's attendance. No refunds are given for late arrivals, early departures, or absence due to child/parent illness.

Remember: Quality Childcare is not expensive....it's **<u>PRICELESS</u>!!!**

Payments are due every Monday for that week. Make Checks payable to **<u>Your Name.</u>**

Typical Rates

Infants (6 weeks-12months) = $160 per week
Toddlers (age 1 year- 2 year)= $140 per week
25 months-5 years (before entering kindergarten)= $135 per week

School Aged children
Kindergarten = $100 a week during school.
Grades 1 + = $75 a week for before and after care.
Non-School Days= $20 a day/$100 per week

Payments are due by Monday(for that week of care). A late charge of $25 will be added for frequent late payments.

Please make checks payable to YOUR NAME
Receipts: For tax purposes, a yearly statement will be provided to each family after January 15th. Weekly or monthly receipts will be provided if requested.

Picking up Your child:
No one other than the parents or designated person will be allowed to pick up your child(ren) without prior arrangement. I must be notified in advance and have written note with the person's name and relationship to the child. I may request a photo ID.

If there is a court order keeping one parent away from the child, I must have a copy of the order on file in my home. Otherwise, I cannot prevent the non-custodial parent from picking up their child.

I am not *allowed* to release a child to anyone who is under the influence of a substance which impairs their driving ability. Other arrangements will need to be made if someone is unable to drive their children safely home.

Open Door Policy: Please feel free to drop in at anytime throughout the day. To ensure safety I may keep the door locked to protect the children, but you may visit anytime.

Children In My Care:
I have a Ramsey County Class A license for Childcare. This means that I have

been approved to care for up to six non-school aged children in my home (plus four school aged children). I have received CPR, First Aid, SIDS, Shaken Baby, and Car Seat Restraints Training.

Daily schedule:
Depending on the needs of the children, schedule times are flexible and may vary.

7:30am-9am Drop-off and free time for the children.
8:00-9 Breakfast
10:30am Morning Juice/snack
10-12pm Group activities, preschool curriculum, or outside play (weather permitting)
12:30pm-1:30pm lunch
1:30pm-1:45pm Story Time
2:00pm-3:15pm Quiet Time
3:15pm-6:00pm Free Playtime/Afternoon snack/Pickup Time

TV viewing:
Any TV viewing will be educational for the children.

Nap time/Rest time: Children will not be forced to sleep, although, they must remain quiet. Cots and bedding are provided but your child is welcome to bring a favorite blanket or stuffed animal. Children under two years old sleep in portable Pack and Play beds.

Behavior Management & Discipline: See Discipline Policy

House Rules:
1- No hitting, biting, pinching, throwing, pushing, hair pulling, or otherwise hurting ourselves or others (keep all feet, hands, and other objects to yourself).
2-Do not break items intentionally.
3-No running, jumping, wrestling, climbing, or rough-housing in the house.
4-Do not pick up the babies or toddlers.
5-No leaving the house or outside boundaries w/o permission
6-No name calling, foul language, or teasing; everyone deserves to be treated with respect
7-All food and drinks shall remain in the kitchen/dining room area/

If a child refuses to cooperate and will not follow my direction, they will receive time outs as a disciplinary action. Frequent problems may be a cause for termination of a contract.

Child Abuse: I am required by law to report any suspected physical, emotional, sexual abuse or neglect.

Meals/Snacks: All meals and snacks will be provided for your child in accordance with the Child Care Food Program. I also provide basic Enfamil with Iron Formula.

Toilet Training: I will be more than happy to help with toilet training for your child, however I ask that you begin the training process at home, over a weekend or a vacation, before starting at daycare. If your child has frequent accidents, I do require pull-ups during quiet-time/nap-time.

Please Please Please send extra clothing.

For school aged children who still have accidents or have problems with constipation and/or Encopresis (soiling due to fecal impaction), please bring extra underwear *and* pants.

Diaper Changes: Diapers are changed every 2-3 hours or more frequently if required.

Parents are responsible for providing:
*Diapers
*Change of clothes-underwear, socks, shorts, pants, and shirts
*Swimsuit/towel in the summer
**Sunscreens, Bug spray, fever and cold medications, diaper ointment, teething medications, etc (if needed-must have med. form filled out and signed)

Toys:
I will have toys available to meet the children's need for fine and gross motor play. Toys may be brought from home ONLY if your child is willing to share the toy and it is understood there is always the possibility of the toy getting lost or broken. I will not be responsible for lost or broken toys.

Water play: I have a sprinkler and a small wading pool for the "*HOT* Summer" days. I will ask for parents to provide bathing suits and towels for these days.

Property Damage:
Respectful treatment of all property, toys, and furniture is expected. Parents may be asked to pay for any destruction of property that their child causes.

Health Matters:
Please keep in mind that I don't allow your child if she/he is sick; I can only care for children with a mild cold-like symptoms (clear runny nose, slight cough, and NO fever). If your child has H1N1 symptoms, they will be sent home and will need to be kept home 24 hours after the symptoms are gone. This flu is very contagious and can be fatal to very young children. Fevers with sore throat are very common symptoms.

If your child is displaying a fever greater than 101(F) or symptoms of a communicable disease,s he/he cannot be brought to my child care home. If your child becomes ill during the time in my care, you will be asked to come get your child unless other arrangements are made to protect the other children.

Medical Emergencies:
For minor injuries like bumps or bruises, I will provide home First Aid. If the injury is more serious (needs stitches, suspected broken bones, etc.) the parents will be notified immediately.
In case of a serious accident or sudden illness requiring medical attention, the following procedures are followed:
1) A phone call is made to 911.
2) Child's parents (or emergency contacts) are called.

Please make sure that all emergency contact info is up to date and correct. Please report changes immediately. If you list a cell phone or pager as your main contact, please make sure they are on at all times while child is in my care.

Pets
Please be a aware that I do have a cat. He very rarely has any contact with the children. He is an indoor cat and is fixed. He is a very loving cat!

No Smoking or Alcohol: There is ****NO SMOKING,**** on the property; inside or out during hours. Alcohol and Drugs are also prohibited.

Photo taking: Documenting of Daycare activities is part of My Daycare program. In this way we can document our experiences, building of friendships, and some memorable times. Parents will be required to give written permission to photograph your child. Parents will receive any photos that are taken of their child(ren).

FINALLY

I am always open to suggestions and feel communication is very important part of this business. If there are any problems or concerns, I encourage you to talk to me about it. If a lengthy conference is needed, a time that is convenient to both of us will be scheduled, as the other children still need my attention during normal business hours. Thank you for the opportunity to work with you and to be part of your child's life. I look forward to the future!

I retain the right to enforce these policies at will. Lack of enforcement of a certain policy at any given time does not indicate that that particular policy is no longer in effect.

I also retain the right to add to this Handbook as needed, if something comes up!

Thanks again-

Your Name
Owner/Operator
Address and Phone Number

_____

Signature of Provider   Date

_____

Signature of Parent(s)   Date